The 9 Habits of Successful Entrepreneurs

What You Should Be Doing to Maximize Your Energy, Save Time, and Enjoy Consistent Wins

RYAN BATTLES

Title: The 9 Habits of Successful Entrepreneurs
Subtitle: What You Should Be Doing to Maximize Your Energy, Save Time, and Enjoy Consistent Wins

ISBN-13: 978-1515008965
ISBN-10: 1515008967

To Grace, Lydia, Benson, and Jack:

Of all of the habits I work on, spending time with you is the most important. I am proud to call you my children.

—Dad

The 9 Habits of Successful Entrepreneurs

CONTENTS

INTRODUCTION TO THE 9 HABITS OF SUCCESSFUL ENTREPRENEURS

We all have habits. Some good, some bad. Do you brush your teeth every morning? That's a good habit most people have formed, which is reinforced by social repercussions for those who fall out of line.

Habits can relate to health, hygiene, relationships, emotional stability, productivity, etc. The amazing things about habits is that they are like the constant drip of water that carves deep path into stone. Small decisions, made everyday, are some of the most powerful forces in our lives.

Over the years, I've paid attention to the habits that people form, especially successful entrepreneurs. What small things are they doing that bring them to the success that they have today?

What small changes can I make in my life, on a regular basis, that will have a dramatic impact on where I end up as an entrepreneur?

This book outlines nine habits that I have discovered are common to some of the world's most successful self-starters. While some of these habits are already at play in many people's lives, few people incorporate all of them without experiencing a great deal of success in one or more areas.

The beautiful thing about these habits is that each and every millionaire entrepreneur started off life without these habits. Each and every one of them were put into practice deliberately, and through practice.

This means that none of these habits are out of your reach. We can all experience their benefits and the success they bring by adding them to our own routines one step at a time.

There was a time when I did not practice any of these habits. Honestly, I'm still working on getting better at most of them. However, even a little bit of time spent in each of these habits yields immediate results.

This book will teach you how to:

- Gain clarity and perspective through meditation (and realize that it isn't as weird as you may think)

- Get way more done in a day by employing time management hacks that leverage natural energy patterns we all experience

- Leverage specific techniques before, during, and after conferences to expand your network, and consequently, your opportunities

- Stay on track and achieve measurable goals by setting up regular personal retreats

- Remain positive and clear your thoughts through journaling practices that only take 5 minutes per day

- Free up more time by outsourcing the right tasks, with a step-by-step guide on what you can outsource and how to get started

- Use exercise as a means towards getting more done, even though it takes a little time out of your day

- Get started with a mastermind group that will be brutally honest with you, and provide the encouragement and accountability to move beyond "good enough"

- Incorporate a morning routine that starts you off on the right foot, giving you the best possible preparation for what lies ahead in the day

None of these happen by themselves, they are all practices that need to be worked on and improved. I will confess, they are not easy to incorporate without some work. Perhaps this is why successful entrepreneurs are in the minority, while people who "have an idea" or "tried something once" are fairly common.

In the research behind this book, I've also strengthened my

own use of the nine habits, and have seen measurable growth in a short period of time. I challenge you to do the same. Don't let this be another book that sits on your digital bookshelf. Start with one habit at a time, and think about how you can start to implement it to a greater degree, and see how quickly you begin to see results.

Bonus Content

In researching these nine habits of successful entrepreneurs, I've also stumbled across five habits that derail entrepreneurs. These habits are all to common, and are often to blame for keeping self-starters from achieving their full potential.

I've made this resource available to you for free, simply head over to https://ryanbattles.com/5-habits to download your copy of *The Five Habits that Derail You as an Entrepreneur.*

Visit https://ryanbattles.com/5-habits for your free copy.

THE HABIT OF MEDITATION

The life of an entrepreneur is often riddled with anxiety, stress, lack of sleep, and an overdose of caffeine. While a fast-paced environment and hard-working attitude are often what leads an entrepreneur to success, over time, it can be the very thing that causes burnout.

A growing trend amongst entrepreneurs is the practice of meditation. Listening to interviews with notable entrepreneurs such as Tim Ferriss and Kevin Rose, I have been hearing more and more how successful founders are relying on the benefits of meditation to keep them grounded in the midst of an often chaotic environment.

Why Meditation is Good for Entrepreneurs

I used to think that meditation was simply for people that lived outside of Western culture, or had a strange spiritual belief system that didn't jive much with my own. Upon further research, it turns out that meditation doesn't have to be a spiritual experience at all (although it is for some), but simply an exercise of the mind to clear thought patterns, focus on a specific word or idea (called a mantra), or simply to observe the thoughts that come to mind when it is relaxed.

To many who practice meditation, the focus is on achieving calmness, and a sense of inner balance. This benefit comes from meditation's ability to train the mind to let go of things that it cannot control, leading to what has been called a "liberated" or "enlightened" life.

For entrepreneurs, meditation can bring about the following benefits:

1. **Relaxed State of Mind** - By spending even 10 minutes in meditation each day, the entrepreneur experiences a brief moment where the demands of the day are put on hold.

2. **Greater Confidence** - By being still and removing distractions, the entrepreneur often gains a deeper perspective that removes the negativity that can be a barrier to self-confidence. Enabling them to take more risks and move forward where others are paralyzed by fear and doubt.

3. **Reduced Stress** - Negative stress is often a byproduct of juggling too much and not taking any time-outs to gain perspective. The discipline of regular meditation forces the entrepreneur to give the mind a "power-nap", refreshing it to handle the demands of the day.

4. **Increased Creativity** - Creativity isn't just for artists, every successful entrepreneur needs to conjure up creative solutions on a regular basis. By starting the day with a prepared mind, the entrepreneur is better equipped to think outside of the box, or let their mind wander towards solutions that might not have come to mind when their stress levels are elevated.

Like physical exercise, the practice of meditation is ironic in that while it takes up some time from your day, in the greater scheme of things it adds time to your day by allowing you to be more efficient and productive with the rest of your day.

Common Types of Meditation

There is no one way to meditate. In fact, a quick search on Google will unearth hundreds of different schools of meditation. For the most part, however, they can be divided into one of two main categories:

1. **Focused Attention Meditation** - In this type of meditation, the mind seeks to focus on a single object, thought, word, or even simply the breaths that are taken. The goal is to clear out everything from the mind that is not a part of this

focus. Sometimes the objects of focus have meaning, while other times words are repeated over and over (such as "om"), and have no meaning other than being a mystic syllable to focus on.

2. **Open Monitoring Meditation** - As opposed to having a focus during meditation, the open monitoring method simply observes whatever thoughts pass through the mind during this time of meditation, letting go of any judgment or attachment to these thoughts. This practice encourages a lack of reaction to thoughts and stimuli, which in turn builds the ability to have more control over reactions outside of meditation.

Some types of meditation, known as "guided meditation", have a teacher or guide that instruct the individual in what to focus on, or when to allow time for open monitoring. This is a great place for many entrepreneurs to start as it requires no research or practice before starting.

Simple Steps to Begin Meditating Today

While some forms of meditation are only taught in paid classes (such as Transcendental Meditation), many forms of meditation take little to no preparation at all. Here are a few basic steps to begin meditating:

1. **Find a Comfortable Position** - This can be sitting on the ground, upright in a chair, or even lying on the ground (although you want to ensure you don't fall asleep). While

certain types of meditation lend better to particular sitting positions due to breathing techniques, the beginner simply needs to be able to relax comfortably.

2. **Listen to a Guided Meditation** - These are available as apps for your smart phone, as YouTube videos, or audio downloads. Check out the resources section at the end of this chapter for specific resources.

3. **Be Patient** - The first few times may feel a little awkward. However, just like physical exercise, the benefits come with consistency.

4. **Slowly Increase Time** - You can't expect to go a 30 minute session on your first one without letting your mind wander. That is why many meditation teachers suggest you start with a short amount of time and gradually increase it.

Resources

Guided Meditation on YouTube

- Guided Meditation Sleep: Delta Waves, Deep Sleep, Inner Peace (https://www.youtube.com/watch?v=txQ6t4yPIM0)

- Breathing Guided Imagery Meditation (https://www.youtube.com/watch?v=BDQKFXeC2Dc)

- 10-Minute Meditation for Anxiety (https://www.youtube.com/watch?v=xoYnqvadurg)

Mobile Applications

- Buddhify (http://buddhify.com/) (iOS & Android)

- Stop, Breathe & Think (https://itunes.ap-ple.com/us/app/stop-breathe-think/id778848692) (iOS)

- The Mindfulness App (http://www.mindapps.se/) (iOS & Android)

Biofeedback Hardware

This is perhaps the most interesting item to feature as a resource, but a $299 bluetooth headband called a Muse (http://www.choosemuse.com/) can detect brain activity, and provides auditory feedback into your headphones, training you to develop effective meditation techniques. Entrepreneurs like Pat Flynn are big proponents of the tool. Pat recently wrote concerning his regular use of the Muse:

When I'm working I can actually catch myself getting off-thought and get back on track faster, and I feel a lot more focused during my work too, especially while writing. -Pat Flynn

While a $299 accessory is not necessary to realize the benefits of meditating, for those of us who love biofeedback and new technology, the Muse is worth a look.

According to the American Psychological Association, even a minor amount of short-lived stress can make an impact on your health (both physical and mental). While entrepreneurs often feel that they need to "go go go" in order to be successful, taking the time out of the day to practice meditation has been a proven, effective method for increasing your productivity throughout the day, providing appropriate perspective, and training to react appropriately to stressors that are inevitable throughout the day.

THE HABIT OF TIME MANAGEMENT

One of the best parts of being an entrepreneur is the ability to work on exactly what you want to work on. The flip side to this privilege is that if you chose to work on the wrong thing, or otherwise poorly manage your time, you miss out on achieving your greatest potential.

We all have the potential for great success, so how do we leverage time management strategies to take us to the next level?

Managing Your Energy

Have you ever had an afternoon where you just couldn't get into the groove and get anything done? Have you ever had a morning where you felt like you achieved 3 days worth of productivity before noon? I've experienced both, and I would say that the biggest difference between those two scenarios is the energy level I experienced in the latter, more productive time.

We always have a 24 hours in a day, but our energy levels can sometimes be high, and sometimes be low. Author Tony Schwartz writes:

"The core problem with working longer hours is that time is a finite resource. Energy is a different story. - Tony Schwartz, author of Be Excellent at Anything

By increasing our energy levels throughout the day, we consequently boost what we can get done in those static 24 hours.

To do this, we must first **recognize our natural energy patterns**. Are you more productive in the morning? Does the afternoon leave you less creative? Do you have greater focus late at night? Once you realize where your peaks and valleys are naturally, you can leverage those to get the most fitting work done at that time. For example, here is my personal natural energy flow:

- **Early Morning:** I'm the most inspired and upbeat. This is a great time to reflect on progress, make plans, or journal.

- **Mid Morning:** I'm the most focused and alert, this is a great time to write a blog post.

- **Late Morning:** I'm starting to think about lunch, so my body is winding down productivity mode. This is a great time for routine tasks, like clearing out the inbox or sending out email responses.

- **Early Afternoon:** My creative energy is much lower than the morning, so I use the afternoon to knock out tasks that were likely put into a list earlier in the morning. For me, this includes programming or other technical work.

- **Late Afternoon:** I get a "the end of the day is near" rush of motivation, and can get a lot done in a short period. This is also great for technical work, or anything that I've been putting off all day because it was not urgent, but still important.

One of the patterns I realize is that I tend to have less energy in the afternoon, so I need to be told what to do (the "early morning" me tells me what to do with a list). This energy is noticeably affected by what I've had to eat for lunch, and how much I've been sitting during the day. By eating a lighter lunch I can provide just enough nutrition to keep me from letting hunger be a distraction, but not too much that fullness makes me tired. Also, by taking perhaps a post-lunch walk or regular breaks from my desk in the afternoon I keep the energy levels up so I can achieve more in the same amount of time.

Commit to a Weekly Plan

As mentioned previously, one of the challenges that entrepreneurs face is making sure the thing that you are working on is what you should be working on. I have found that writing out my plan for the week has been one of the greatest productivity boosters in my arsenal.

Making sure that each day has a task or two that must be done in order to reach my goals ensures that I work on the important, not just what I feel like doing for the day. Entrepreneur James Clear states:

"If you do the most important thing first, then you'll never have a day when you didn't get something important done." – James Clear

On Sunday evening, I open a text document and write out each of the days of the week. For each of those days I write down at least one thing that I need to accomplish that day in order to reach my weekly goals. There have been weeks where I skipped this step due to the business of life, and I feel it throughout the week until I sit down and plan out a task for the remaining days in the week. The unplanned weeks are the ones I waste the most time on the non-essential tasks that jump in front of me, and I don't end up any closer to my goals.

This tip can be expanded out from a weekly plan to a monthly plan, which gives each week a few concrete jobs to accomplish, or a yearly plan that gives each month a specific set of goals.

Free up Time With Essentialism

Recently I have heard many entrepreneurs talking about a book by Greg McKeown called *Essentialism: The Disciplined Pursuit of Less*. Essentially, McKeown strikes a nerve by calling out our frequent inability to discern what is absolutely essential, and eliminate the rest. He reminds us that when we say "yes" by agreeing to that meeting, reading and responding to all of those emails, and getting distracted by whatever is in front of our eyes, we empower others to set our agenda:

"Remember that if you don't prioritize your life someone else will." -Greg McKeown

My favorite saying in this regard is "If it isn't a 'Hell Yes', then it is a 'no'". Someone want to grab coffee? A small project come across your plate? What is your gut feeling when you receive this request?

Of course, this bears some disclaimer. You can be an amazing essentialist and lose all of your friends and network. However, this doesn't mean that you have to say "yes" to everything in order to maintain friendships and professional relationships–you just need to say "yes" to only the essentials. Perhaps meeting for coffee once a month instead of once a week is in order. Perhaps saying "no" to that small project opens up your time to work on something that will be more of a game-changer.

Lookout for the 80/20

In 1896, Italian economist Vilfredo Pareto published a paper explaining that roughly 80% of the land in Italy was owned by 20% of the population. He also noticed that about 20% of the pea pods in his garden produced 80% of the pea yield. The point is, in many areas of life, there is a minority that produces the majority, while the majority produces the minority.

The exact ratio of 80/20 is not an absolute ratio by any means, and in some cases it might be 95/5, or 75/25. However, it is important to note in what ways this principle plays out in how you spend your time.

- What are the 80% of tasks that only move you forward 20%?

- What are the 20% of activities over the past year that have given you nearly 80% of your success?

- What are the 20% of the people in your network that give you 80% of the encouragement and motivation?

- What are the 20% of the projects or activities that provide 80% of your income?

- Who are the 20% of customers that provide you 80% of your income?

Once you identify the minority that has the majority of the effect, you can spend your time and energy investing in those people and activities in order to maximize effectiveness. Author Stephen Covey writes:

"The key is in not spending time, but in investing it." – Stephen R. Covey

We all spend 24 hours a day whether we want to or not. How we spend that time is another matter, and some tasks clearly provide more return than others.

Time Boxing with Pomodoro

When you have 4 hours to accomplish what appears to be 5

hours of work, you get that work done in 4 hours. When you have 10 hours to accomplish the same tasks, you somehow find a way to allow it to take 10 hours. We are wired to work faster under constraints. That is the concept that Francesco Cirillo leveraged in the late 1980s when he introduced the "Pomodoro Method".

"Pomodoro" is the Italian word for tomato, the shape of a common kitchen timer in many kitchens. Cirillo explained that we can accomplish more by setting a timer for a fixed amount of time (traditionally 25 minutes), and working on a specific task during that time. After that session (referred to as "a pomodoro"), you take a short 3-5 minute break. After four pomodori, you take a longer 15-20 minute break.

Of course, not every task can be accomplished within a 25 minute sprint, so some tasks might be broken up into multiple pomodori. With this method, you know that you can't stop what you are doing to make a quick phone call, or check your email. If your mind remembers that you are going to start a composting pile after work, you don't stop what you are doing to research composting piles. Speaker and author Zig Ziglar states:

Lack of direction, not lack of time, is the problem. We all have twenty-four hour days." – Zig Ziglar

By planning out the tasks to be done, and giving them dedicated sprints of work, we force upon ourselves a sense of urgency throughout the day. That same sense of urgency that I mentioned before makes me more productive from 4:00pm - 5:00pm, knowing that the end of the day is near and I need to kick it into high gear.

This time-boxing technique can also extend into other creative practices, like shifting your location throughout the day. Instead of spending the whole day at the office, try giving yourself 2 hours at the coffee shop in the morning to accomplish a certain task, then heading over to the library for another 2 hour sprint for another task. Knowing that you have a certain time frame to accomplish a certain task, then taking a short break and either driving to another location or walking around to give your brain some extra oxygen is a surefire way to ensure that you accomplish more than you would by simply sitting down for an 8 hour stretch and working at a leisurely pace.

Reduce Friction with Batching

Does your workday involve a variety of tasks? Take note of how much time it takes to transition from activity to activity. For example, when I make a phone call, I get out paper for notes, put in my earpieces, and find a quiet location. If I made all of my phone calls for the day at once, I only have to do that once, instead of random times throughout the day. Speaker and author Michael Hyatt shares:

Working in a perpetual state of shifting tasks and refocusing attention creates fatigue, stress, and decreased productivity. -Michael Hyatt

The benefits of batching can be applied on a weekly level as well. For example, some people schedule all of their phone calls or meetings for a particular day each week. John Lee Dumas has a daily podcast, but he records all 7 of his episodes each week in one day. Whether it is on a weekly or daily level, batching similar tasks together reduces the friction of shifting activities and saves time.

Prioritize with GTD

All of these time-saving techniques are useless if you aren't working on the tasks that need to be done. The best book I've read by far in regards to planning out your daily tasks is David Allen's *Getting Things Done: The Art of Stress-Free Productivity* (the methods of which are often shortened to "GTD"). Allen outlines a method of getting ideas and tasks out our heads and into an actionable system. According to Allen:

"Your mind is for having ideas, not holding them." — David Allen

Allen instructs his clients to first do a mental dump of all of the tasks floating around in their head. Whether it is on paper or within task management software. Next, his clients set up a single inbox where all of the tasks moving forward need to be dumped into for processing. This could be a physical bin, a computer folder, or a section of the task management software. From there, each task can have one of the following applied:

- **Do it**: If it takes less than 2 minutes, just do it.

- **Defer it**: Put it on the calendar or under a project list to be acted upon later.

- **Delegate it**: Assign someone else the responsibility of completing the task.

With GTD, you also need to have a weekly review to check over the active projects that are on your lists, and choose which ones are going to be worked on next.

This is definitely an over-simplification of the system, but the point is that your mind is no place to organize all of these tasks and priorities without writing them down first. When you write them down, and regularly review these tasks, you can be sure that nothing slips through the cracks, and your attention is given to the important tasks that get results.

Imagine a couple of 30 year olds who grew up in the same neighborhood with similar family situations. One goes on to build and launch a company that gets acquired for millions of dollars on his 29th birthday, and one ends up working a 9-5 corporate job for decent pay, but has no savings and generally hates his workweek. Assuming that they both had the same opportunities presented to them from the start, the key difference between them is how they spent those years between childhood and 30 years old. They both had the same amount of time, how they spent it was the difference.

Perhaps your goal is less about monetary gain and more about quality of life, time spent with family and friends, or the ability to travel without time restraints. Whatever your life's goals, consistently applying time management strategies will ensure that you make maximum progress towards them, instead of getting distracted and working towards the wrong goals, or worse yet, towards nothing at all.

THE HABIT OF ATTENDING CONFERENCES

Conferences are an investment. Just like placing your money in a 401K, spending time and money on a conference can pay dividends many times the costs. The key is, you have to approach them the right way. If you view conferences as simply heading to a major city and listening to a few slideshow presentations, then you are missing out on some amazing opportunities for growth.

It's Not About the Teaching

I've been to conferences where the teaching was absolutely amazing. In fact, when I went to the BaconBiz Conference in Philadelphia, I filled out half a notebook during the talks. I was definitely inspired. However, that information that I gathered has also been shared in numerous podcasts interviews, blog articles, business books, and YouTube videos. In fact, at many conferences, you can view some of the talks from a previous year for free!

Perhaps you need a concentrated few days to sit and listen to all of this information, and that's certainly a way to receive value from attending a conference. However, I like to focus on what cannot be gathered any other way, something that can only happen at a conference: the networking.

A conference provides a unique opportunity for a large number of people, away from work, with similar interests to mingle and get to know each other. The type of networking I'm talking about is not simply running around distributing your business card to as many people as possible. In fact, I suggest not even using business cards (you'll see why here in a bit). Conferences involve learning together, processing that learning, sharing experiences, and hanging out during meals and evening activities.

There is no way to know exactly how the networking opportunities will turn out at a conference. In fact, I've always been surprised by the positive experiences that have come my way due to speaking to the right people at conferences. When I say "the right people", you have no way of knowing who these people are. While we would all love to have some uninterrupted time with some of the keynote speakers, it might just be the unassuming person next to you that is looking for someone like you to work with on a lucrative project. Perhaps that person will be the one to respond when you are looking for a new job, and wants to recommend you to their supervisor. You never know, you can't expect it, all you can do is put yourself out there and be intentional about taking advantage of the conference.

Before the Conference

Before you even step foot in the conference venue, there are plenty of activities that can prime the pump for effective networking opportunities.

- **Follow the conference hashtag on Twitter** and engage with people who are posting how excited they are to go to the conference. Many people post an update when they've purchased their plane or conference ticket. Hit reply and let them know that you are going too and are looking forward to connecting.

- **Sign up for the conference page on Lanyrd**. If there isn't a conference page, you can create one. Lanyrd is a social conference directory, where attendees can connect and see who else is coming. Get to know a few names and faces on that list, and send them a quick tweet letting them know that you're looking forward to connecting at the conference. When you get there, you'll have less names to memorize since you've done a little homework beforehand.

- **Email the speakers** and let them know that you are looking forward to hearing their talks. Even better, share with them why you are looking forward to their talks. It helps as a speaker to know why people will be excited about your talk, and perhaps what you should emphasize during the presentation. Besides that, they may remember the note if you get a chance to meet them, and will instantly break the ice and open doors for a conversation.

Some of these things may be out of your comfort zone, but trust me, nobody is going to find any of the above practices annoying, as it is our human nature to be flattered when people notice us, desire to connect with us, and are looking forward to hearing our talks. They may not recall the tweet or email, so don't be offended or dejected if you mention it and they can't remember, just move on and start a conversation anyway. You never know where it will lead.

During the Conference

Make sure you get to the conference the day before it begins. Many others will be doing this and often will be looking for a group of people to hang out with. Follow the conference's hashtag on Twitter to keep an eye out for tweets like:

Heading to X for dinner with a couple folks if anyone from #conference wants to join.

Send a quick reply that you'll meet them there, and show up. If you don't see any tweets like that, create one of your own. Remember, there ARE going to be people there without anyone to talk to, and you could be that connection. This will give you a few familiar faces the next day when you attend the conference.

During the conference presentations, I suggest using a notebook and pen to take notes, and leaving your laptop or notepad in the hotel room. This will prevent you from going down a rabbit hole online when you could be paying attention to the speaker. If you have a smartphone, you can still be reached for emergencies, and can check email for something urgent if needed. Not having your laptop also frees you up to move about the room without lugging it around, or worry about setting it down and walking away.

Between talks, don't be the person who dives into their phone's screen for the next 15 minutes. I'm always amazed at the people I see on their phones and computers between sessions. I know that a small percentage of them might have a fire that they need to put out at work, but for the majority, they would do better to close the laptop and walk up to a stranger and extend a hand to shake. People wear name-tags at conferences for a reason, we're supposed to mingle!

While getting to know new people, make sure that you start off by asking them questions about themselves. Pushing your own agenda, no matter how interesting it might be, can come off as self-centered. If they ask you first, then feel free to share, but if you kick off the conversation, focus on them. If they are polite, they will in return ask you. If they never ask you about yourself, then they are unlikely to be helpful in other matters anyway.

The Alternative Business Card

I mentioned previously that I don't bring business cards to conferences. When someone asks for a business card, I reply:

I don't have any on me, but what is your email so I can follow up with you after the conference?

Write this email down. They may hand you one of their business cards, or they may just tell you. The key is, the ball is now in your court to send them an email and share your contact information, after all of the hubbub of the conference has died down, and they have more time to process your connection and perhaps even begin talks about something mutually beneficial. If I would have just handed them a card, it likely would have ended up in a mass of other cards, and I wouldn't have a good reason to reach out to them after the conference.

After the Conference

Many conferences have an after-party. I definitely recommend hitting that if you can, but it is also common for people to start taking off to head home that evening to skip another hotel night fee. If I am attending a conference on the West Coast, I try to catch a red-eye flight back so I can stay late, save on the hotel room, and get home at a decent time the next morning.

Just like before the conference, post-conference is a great opportunity to email the speakers and let them know how their talks impacted you. If you have a chance to put something that they shared into practice, even better. Let them know that you took their advice and what impact it had on you.

As mentioned before, this is also a great time to follow-up with those you met at the conference that you need to share your contact information with. You can also post messages to Twitter with the conference's hashtag mentioning a few of the people that you enjoyed hanging out with, or reflect on a fond memory you had of the conference.

Becoming a Speaker

Conferences can take on a whole new face when you become a speaker. As such, you not only get to attend the conference for free, but you'll have an instant ice-breaker with folks that you meet who saw your talk.

Many conferences have a call to speakers, where you can submit a proposal to speak. I suggest throwing three potential topics out there, as there will be a greater chance that one will be chosen. For conferences that don't have a call to speakers, you can always email the organizers and let them know that you are interested in speaking, and what their selection process is like. Some larger conferences only allow big-names in to speak, so it is better to make a name for yourself starting with the smaller conferences. If you are good, and people are interested in what you share, you will eventually get more speaking opportunities.

Conferences provide a unique opportunity to get away from work, concentrate on learning, and network with other like-minded individuals. You can never predict just how a connection is going to turn beneficial, in fact, most don't amount to much more than a nice 10 minutes shared together. However, for that one connection that ends up landing you that new job, that new client, or inspiring you to take the next step towards your goals, the value can be many times more than what you paid to attend the conference. The key is: be pro-active, be intentional, and step out of your comfort zone in order to make the most out of attending a conference.

THE HABIT OF PERSONAL RETREATS

Taking regular personal retreats is one of the best habits you can develop to ensure the health of your business.

Now, you may be thinking, "I don't have the time for a personal retreat", or "I have kids", or "I have a day job I can't just take time away from."

These are valid reasons, but each and every one of them can be overcome. Once you see how beneficial a personal retreat is to your business and personal life, you will wonder how you ever functioned without them.

In this chapter, we'll be looking at what exactly is a personal retreat, what do people do on a personal retreat, and how can you fit one in when you have other commitments that make it difficult to take time away in solitude.

I Don't Need a Personal Retreat, I'm Doing Just Fine

Why do we even need a personal retreat?

I used to think this way. I'd hear people take personal retreats and I'd say "must be nice". I can't do that, I've got four young kids!

Well, there are actually a handful of benefits that an entrepreneur experiences when taking a personal retreat:

1. **A personal retreat allows you to gain perspective.** Perspective helps move your business forward. Whereas meditation helps you to gain perspective during your day, a personal retreat provides prospective for the next few months and beyond.

2. **A personal retreat is a discipline.** The act of stopping and reflecting is not something we do naturally, especially entrepreneurs. We are often so excited to move a project forward that the act of pausing takes conscious effort. A personal retreat forces us to stop, unplug, and make decisions that will greatly impact the future of our businesses.

3. **A personal retreat prevents stagnation.** A good personal retreat will inspire you to set a few goals for the next few months. This forces us into a time-crunch to complete certain activities, moving the business forward.

Taking a personal retreat is not easy, it does require some scheduling and perhaps even a little money if an overnight is involved. However, the time and money spent is more than recouped if your personal retreat helps you to take your business to the next level.

It's amazing how little time we spend in reflection on our businesses. In *Essentialism*, Greg McKeown writes:

"Sometimes we spend more time planning our vacation than planning our careers." -Greg McKeown

When we go on vacation, not only do we often create a list to ensure that we don't forget anything, but we get our affairs in order as well.

We stop the mail, we arrange for someone to keep an eye on the house, we mark our calendars, we clear our schedules. If we can do it for our personal vacations, we can certainly do it for a personal retreat.

So How Long is this Personal Retreat Supposed to Be?

Depending on who you talk to, a personal retreat can last anywhere from a single workday to a whole week. Many people find two days to be ideal.

Rob Walling, founder of Drip recently did an "Ask Me Anything" thread on Bootstrappers.io, and had this to say about his personal retreats:

"The ideal length is 48 hours or longer (totally solo, no family, no kids). This also means you need to feel like you have plenty of time to make this successful. So don't make the trip too short. I recommend 48 hours." -Rob Walling

In contrast Greg McKeown calls his reflection time "Quarterly Offsites", and does them every three months, for a part of the workday.

Depending on the level of decision-making, prioritizing, and de-stressing you need to do, your length and frequency of a retreat will vary.

For me, I have four young children and a wife that works part-time. Getting away for several days is a big ask from my wife, so I have elected to go the 1-day quarterly personal retreat schedule.

I like the quarterly retreat because it forces me to set three-month goals, which is usually a long-enough time to finish something meaningful, but short enough that I don't procrastinate. I might even break down my quarterly goal into monthly achievables, which I then visit when making my weekly plan every Sunday night.

What Is the Agenda of a Personal Retreat?

The last thing you want to do is go on a personal retreat and waste time not getting deep into the things that need to be thought through.

It definitely helps to have an agenda going into the retreat so you know what to reflect upon.

Part 1: Reflection

I always kick my retreats off by reflecting the time since the last retreat:

1. What have I accomplished since my last retreat?

2. What has worked well for me since my last retreat?

3. How do I feel about what I've accomplished since my last retreat?

4. What am I thankful for since my last retreat?

5. What could I have done differently since my last retreat?

Part 2: Stillness

I think this step is critical. After clearing out your thoughts from the period since your last retreat, try to spend some time just being aware of your thoughts.

Enjoy a break from all of the distractions of your daily life. Your email, Twitter, your children interrupting you.

Just…relax.

Another great activity during this time is to take a walk. If you are out in nature, head out on a trail. Get moving so your brain can enjoy the increase of oxygen, and who knows what thoughts might enter your mind.

If you are a person of faith, this could be a great time to spend in prayer. Ask for clarity and wisdom as you move into the planning period.

Part 3: Planning

By now you should be ready to sit down and start planning out the next period between retreats. Here are a few questions that might be helpful to explore during this time:

1. What would make this next period awesome?

2. Where do I see myself in the next 2 years?

3. How can this next period help me achieve those long-term goals?

4. What events are coming up that I need to prepare for?

5. How can I break my goals up into monthly blocks?

6. What will I get started on in the next week?

7. What could potentially prevent me from achieving these goals?

Hopefully by the end of reflecting upon these questions you will have a pretty good idea of what you'll be trying to accomplish over the next few months until your next retreat.

Are There Any Ideal Locations for a Retreat?

While there are dedicated retreat centers located throughout the country, you can have an effective retreat often within an hour's drive or so from where you currently live.

Even in a big city there are metroparks and quiet libraries for hiking and journaling. Perhaps a little noise helps you to reflect, so a downtown coffee shop might be a good spot for an afternoon.

If you're taking a multi-day retreat, look for cabin rentals or rooms near a lake, ocean, forest, desert, mountains, or river.

To Unplug or Not?

This is a tough one:

Should you bring your laptop to a personal retreat?

Some people like to go in with just a notebook and a few pens. Some people bring their full technology stack with them.

Personally, I like having my laptop with me to dump my goals into my task management software. However, during my reflection time, it is just me and a notebook.

It is during this "unplugged" time that I gain most of my insight. Arianna Huffington (co-founder of the Huffington Post) states:

Your performance will actually improve if you can commit to not only working hard, but also unplugging, recharging and renewing yourself. -Arianna Huffington

If having your laptop will become a distraction that prevents you from really getting away, then I would suggest not bringing it. If you can limit its use to only that which benefits your implementation of insight gained during the retreat, then go ahead and bring it.

My Last Retreat's Itinerary

The last time I took a personal retreat, I utilized a 1-day schedule and told my wife I'd be coming home late for dinner. I started the day off earlier than normal in order to maximize the potential of the day.

- **6:00** - Headed to Starbucks for a wake-me-up and to start journaling on the previous three months.

- **8:00** - Headed to the Metropark for some hiking and time to let my thoughts organize themselves from the morning's reflection time.

- **10:30** - Headed to a French bakery I love for a fresh croissant. This is one of those pleasures I don't enjoy very often, so I wanted to have something to look forward to mid-morning.

- **11:00** - Got in my car and drove to the conservatory. This retreat was during the winter time, so I wanted to feel rejuvenated by entering the lush, humid rainforest room. It was here that I took a seat and spent some time in deep thought and stillness.

- **12:30** - Enjoyed lunch and reading.

- **1:30** - Headed to the lobby at the Hilton (plenty of tables and chairs, fireplace). Did my future planning and goal setting.

- **4:00** - Headed to another metropark for a final hike to let any final thoughts go through processing and settle in.

- **5:30** - Stopped in to the local library to whip out my laptop and put my final reflections into my task management software. I also put my goals on the calendar as a reminder.

- **6:30** - Feeling rejuvenated and inspired with the plans for the next three months, I headed home.

Taking time away for a personal retreat is a discipline that not many professionals take seriously enough. We have enough going on in our daily lives that a break "just to think" sounds pretty unproductive. However, it is during those breaks in our routine that we discover whether or not what we are being productive in is what really matters.

We can utilize this time to ensure that our ships are on the right course, and that we are not missing any major opportunities that are right in front of us.

Taking time out to think is perhaps one of the best uses of our time as entrepreneurs.

THE HABIT OF JOURNALING

The human brain is the most complex structure in the universe. With it we solve equations, write poetry, and recall our first days of school.

Because the brain is so complex, we often have a hard time juggling so many thoughts throughout our day, and end up overwhelmed, lacking clarity, or simply unable to process the jumble of inputs, floating thoughts and ideas.

Fortunately, we can use tools to help our thoughts sort themselves out, one of the most effective being a journal.

The Benefits of Journaling

Journaling is not simply writing a letter to yourself at the end of the day, recalling the days events. This is a *diary*, and is simply one type of journal.

At it's heart, journaling is simply taking the experiences, reflections, and ideas that are in your head, and writing them down.

By putting your thoughts into written word, you engage in a creative process that allows you to brainstorm effective solutions and explore new lines of thinking.

It is no wonder that journaling is a habit effective entrepreneurs make a part of their routine. Few things come close to providing the clarity of thought and organizing of the mind that journaling can provide.

The good news is, journaling doesn't have to be a time-consuming process. It could be as simple as jotting down a few reflections during your morning cup of coffee.

Recipe for Simple Journaling

One of the simplest journaling practices is simply doing a little reflection on the past, positive thinking to increase happiness, and planning for the day to promote growth.

Exercise - Tomorrow morning, take out a sheet of paper and answer the following questions before you start your day:

1. What was something awesome about yesterday?

2. What was something that could have been improved yesterday?

3. What is something that you are thankful for today?

4. What would make today great?

Journaling the answers to these four questions on a regular basis will provide you with the necessary reflection and planning needed to make better decisions as an entrepreneur, increasing clarity and mindfulness.

Journaling As-Needed

Besides a routine of journaling, sometimes it is just helpful to write out reflections on a specific topic that is floating around in your head. I know for myself I often am paralyzed by a decision or upcoming situation, and one of the only solutions is to simply sit down with a notebook and hash out my thoughts into words.

Examples of times when as-needed journaling can be effective:

1. **When you need to weigh your options.** This is where the classic "pros and cons" list can be effective. Yes, that is a form of journaling. You are simply committing your thoughts about an option to words. Many times the answer becomes clearer when you write out the outcomes of a decision.

2. **When you begin to feel overwhelmed.** Sometimes we have so much going on in our lives that we can't organize it all in our heads. For me, that is when I feel overwhelmed. To combat this, I simply do a brain dump of all the ideas or responsibilities that I have, and organize them. If they are actions that need to be taken, I delegate them to a day or time on the calendar, then forget about them. I can then rest

easy knowing that all of those thoughts are now handled, and there is an appropriate time designated to getting them done.

3. **When you need to reflect to improve the future.** Every three months I take a quarterly retreat to reflect upon the last three months, and journaling is an important part of this process. In journaling I write out what has worked and was hasn't…what I could have changed and what was out of my control. Most importantly, I set goals for the next three months. All of this takes the form of journal entries that I convert into lists later on.

4. **When you need to make a plan.** Have a large responsibility on your shoulders? Do you need to strategize for a project? Journaling is a great way to brainstorm potential paths to completing a task, and often provides the clarity of thought needed to lay out what the necessary steps are to ensure success. As entrepreneurs, we often need to use this type of as-needed journaling to plan out a marketing push, or new feature for our products.

5. **When you need to process a situation.** Sometimes our perception of a situation can cripple us. Whether it is something that has happened in the past or is coming in the future, we can sometimes over or under-react in a way that is not healthy. Journaling helps to provide perspective on a situation, and assists our brains in properly processing it in a way that fosters a healthy outlook. This in-turn reduces

stress, which allows us to function better and get more done.

The beauty of journaling is that it can be messy, and that's okay. With journaling, you don't have to follow any pattern or rules, you can just write what comes into your head. The more free we allow our thoughts to be, the more effective the process of journaling becomes.

Paper or Screen?

Journaling purists will tell you to only use paper when journaling, but many of us type so much faster than we write, that using our keyboards can be a great way to dump our thoughts into words for processing.

For me, there are times I prefer paper journaling, and times I prefer to type it out. I don't think that one way is truly better than the other.

Fortunately, there are a variety of journaling tools out there to get started with:

The Free Ones

I'm honestly a big fan of simply using the default Notes app on my Mac for simple journaling. It can sync across my phone, computer, and tablet instantaneously.

If you're looking for a more robust option, then Evernote is a free, cross-platform solution for maintaining a synchronized journal.

Journaling Apps

If you are interested in a dedicated journaling app, one that highlights dates of entry and provides thought-provoking questions for you, then you might want to search your device's app store for a journaling app.

I'm partial to the Apple ecosystem, so I've enjoyed using Day One, an app for both the desktop and iOS.

I like how Day One has built-in notifications that nudge me to write an entry for the day. There are also a handful of additional features that are not necessary, but kind of nice to have (such as auto-tagging your location where you wrote it, and a passcode lock to maintain privacy).

Paper Journals

If you are going to go the paper route, I enjoy a sketch book as there are no line rules, so if part of my journaling includes a mind map or flowchart, I can just draw those in unimpeded by existing lines.

The Five Minute Journal

A physical journal that has been getting a lot of positive feed-back lately is called The Five Minute Journal.

The journal is meant to be used twice a day, and has the same questions for each entry:

Morning

- I am grateful for…

- What would make today great?

- Daily affirmations, I am…

Evening

- 3 Amazing things that happened today…

- How could I have made today better?

It is printed and bound in a high-quality package, complete with ribbon bookmark, and costs $22.95.

I have one personally, and have enjoyed the simplicity of it. There's never a need to remember what to journal about since it is all laid out for you.

Public Journaling

Sometimes it makes sense to release your journal publicly to the world. Whether it is for accountability, or just to share with others who may be going through the same thing, you can use a blog as a platform to journal out your thoughts. My friend Josh Doody did exactly this when he was working on overcoming the fear of launching a product.

"It helps to write things so I'm forced to think deeply about them. If I know someone else might read it, that adds another layer because I also need to be sure to write clearly." - Josh Doody

No matter whether you write down your reflections and thoughts on paper or screen, the action of putting words to your thoughts opens up a creative process that provides insight and clarity in a way that few other exercises can. It is exactly this insight that empowers many successful entrepreneurs to rise to the top.

THE HABIT OF OUTSOURCING TASKS

One of the key personality traits of an Entrepreneur is that we like to hustle, try new things, and fill our workday with variety. A negative side-effect of this is that we also have a hard time giving up control.

As an entrepreneur, it is imperative that we learn to delegate certain tasks to others.

Without delegation, the sad truth is that we stall the growth of our companies because there is only so much time, energy, and creative focus we can provide as an individual. By outsourcing certain tasks to others, we open up more of our own resources to focus on generating income.

Let's dive into the benefits of outsourcing, why today's economy is primed for an outsourced workforce, which tasks to outsource, which ones to keep in-house, and a step-by-step guide to finding high-quality outsourced talent.

Benefits of Outsourcing

One of the items that keeps entrepreneurs from delegating tasks is that they don't want to hire a workforce. There is some validity to this position, as a workforce requires quite a few added costs to running a business. Hiring a small team of contractors can be beneficial for the following reasons:

- **You pay only for what you need** - A full-time employee needs about 40 hours of work during the week to stay busy. Sometimes you don't need someone to spend that much time on an ongoing basis for certain roles. An example of this would be contracting a lawyer when starting out your business. You certainly don't need (and can't afford) a full-time in-house lawyer, so working with one on a contract basis makes the most sense.

- **Skip the payroll & tax headache** - Hiring a contractor is relatively straight-forward. You pay them, and tell the IRS about it at the end of the year. They are responsible for filing their own taxes and getting their accounting in order.

- **No benefits required** - Many competitive workplaces offer health care, gym memberships, hardware and software, paid time off, etc. In general, none of these things are offered to outsourced help, nor are they expected to be.

- **No space needed** - Depending on the type of business you are running, hiring a workforce requires larger office space, more desks and equipment, etc. A contractor typically works from their own space, or if they must set up in your offices, only need a temporary workspace.

- **Forces you to refine processes** - When hiring a contractor, you are forced to put certain expectations and processes down for them to follow. When this happens you often are encouraged to streamline processes.

- **Forces you to prioritize tasks** - Deciding which tasks to outsource is a process that forces you to list out the tasks that are best performed by you, and which ones should have less of a priority when it comes to your time.

Of course, these benefits are positioned against hiring out for these same tasks. If you decide to do everything yourself, you avoid the office space, tax issues, etc. However, as mentioned previously, you limit yourself to what 1 person can accomplish. Very few successful entrepreneurs got to where they are now without delegating out certain tasks to free them up to work on the business.

Why Today is the Best Time to Outsource

There used to be a time when people would stay with a single company from initial hire to retirement. This no longer holds true for a lot of professionals. In fact, some professionals view self-employment as the only stable option in today's economy.

The result? **Many more highly-qualified professionals are working as contractors** as opposed to sticking it out in the corporate world.

Add this to the fact that it has never been easier to work remotely thanks to modern communication apps:

- Slack (https://slack.com/) for real-time chat

- Skype (http://www.skype.com/) for free video calls

- Dropbox (https://www.dropbox.com/) for sharing documents

- Clever Checklist (http://cleverchecklist.com/) to share processes and requirements

What to Outsource

Which tasks should you be outsourcing? Coming up with a list of tasks to outsource might seem like a daunting task, but essentially it starts with defining your core competencies as a business, and what you've defined as your competitive advantage.

For example, a company such as Apple would never outsource product design…it is what defines them as a company and is one of their key competitive advantages. However, they have outsourced advertising campaigns for these products because advertising is not their key competitive advantage.

Once you define your core competencies as a business, you can start to take note of the tasks that you spend time and energy on, and ask yourself, is my core competency affected if I outsource this?

In most businesses, bookkeeping and legal are not core competencies, so these are usually the first to be outsourced.

Next comes other auxiliary roles, such as writer, designer, developer, project manager, editor, social media, event planner.

Another reason to outsource is if there is a limited-scope task that would benefit from a specialist's input. For example, you might contract a social media specialist to help set up a plan for social media. Perhaps you'll meet with this person every three months in order to analyze and improve this strategy, meanwhile a lower-paid contractor is the one implementing this strategy.

There is a role for consultants and freelancers of all levels even with a small business.

What Not to Outsource

Just as there are certain things that you should definitely outsource, there are also items that should most definitely be done in house.

As mentioned previously, anything that is related to your core competency should not be outsourced. Anything that gives you a competitive advantage should come from within, otherwise your competition is only a freelancer away from matching or beating that advantage.

You should also not outsource items simply because you do not like doing them. For example, many entrepreneurs are tempted to outsource sales right off the bat because they do not like selling. However, even though sales are uncomfortable, we tend to get better at it with time. In fact, for some entrepreneurs, having sales conversations with potential clients will drive product direction and give a clearer picture of your target audience's needs and pain points. Yes, there will come a time when the founder should not be doing sales calls, but it isn't simply because they don't enjoy it.

Finally, you shouldn't outsource tasks that need a full-time person to handle. A 40-hour a week contractor starts to look a lot like an employee to the IRS after a while. If the IRS interprets your contractor relationship as an employer/employee relationship, you could be liable for that person's social security taxes, as well as other costs and penalties.

How to Find Outsourced Talent

The absolute best way to find outsourced talent is to look for recommendations within your own network. Ask your connections on LinkedIn, Facebook, and Twitter if anyone recommends a contractor for the job you are looking to outsource.

If you strike out within your own network, there are a variety of sites that have a database of individuals available for hire, everywhere from $5 to over $100/hr:

- Upwork (https://www.upwork.com/)

- Fiverr (https://www.fiverr.com/)

- Freelancer (https://www.freelancer.com)

- Ask Sunday (http://www.asksunday.com/)

- Virtual Assistant Board (http://virtualassistant-board.com/)

Searching through the sites above you will likely be over-whelmed with the number of people available, how do you separate the wheat from the chaff?:

1. First of all, start by creating a **one-time job** that will represent the type of work your contractor will do. If you are looking for a website designer, ask them to redesign your current homepage. If you are looking for a blog writer, ask them for an article on a given topic.

2. Ask the applicants to **follow a random instruction** when applying. For example, when posting a job on Upwork, in your job description as the applicants to start off their application with the word "tangerine" at the top to show that they read the whole job description.

3. Schedule a **10-min Skype call** with your qualified applicants. This will not only help you see if they can show up for something on time, without technical difficulty, but also helps to weed out any communication issues that you might have further down the road.

4. Finally, to narrow down your final choice: **pay multiple workers to complete the same job**. Yes, you are essentially wasting money here, but not really. The cost of paying for

one more homepage redesign pales in comparison to the cost associated with hiring the wrong person for the job.

Hopefully after these four steps the right candidate for the job will become obvious. While finding the best talent is a tedious and time-consuming process, the benefits far outweigh the due diligence work required in order to find the right person to help run your business.

Outsourcing work is something that many new entrepreneurs are hesitant to try, but the most successful entrepreneurs swear by.

Hiring contractors frees you up to focus on the core competencies that move your business forward, as opposed to the mundane tasks that should be left to others. In addition, hiring an expert to cover specialized areas where appropriate allows us to grow in ways that one person could not grow a company alone.

THE HABIT OF EXERCISE

As an entrepreneur, you are responsible for a lot. Whether it is employees, customers, vendors, marketing tasks, sales, strategic planning...

...Need I go on?

Many times the last thing we feel that we can make time for is exercise. Already we are stretched in a number of directions, who can take an hour out of each day to throw in another that, at first glance, doesn't even improve the bottom line?

The irony of exercise for entrepreneurs is that, even though it takes time out of your day, in the end you actually get more done in the remaining time that you come out ahead.

This chapter is going to dive into the reasons why entrepreneurs become more successful when they exercise regularly, some simple exercises that you can do during the workday from your office, and a few examples of successful entrepreneurs that share their secrets to keeping fit amidst a hectic workday.

Entrepreneur-specific Reasons for Exercising

1. **Entrepreneurs can work out whenever they want.** For the most part, an entrepreneur has control over how they spend their day. Few corporate employees can take a couple hours out for lunch in order to fit a workout in, or leave the office early to work out before heading home.

2. **Exercising is one of the few areas of life you can control.** 50% of small businesses fail within their first five years, but 100% of the business owners who exercise regularly improve their health assuming all else remains the same. Use the laws of biology to your advantage, take heart in the fact that every exercise is an improvement in your overall health.

3. **Exercise fuels your creative juices.** A 2012 study by the Montreal Heart Institute showed aerobic exercise increased cognitive function. To put it bluntly: exercise makes you smarter. Entrepreneurs often place priority on learning and professional development, regular exercise will help them process and retain more.

"If I were to stop exercising because I felt that being a good business owner was a higher priority, then ironically I would end up a worse business owner than I was when it was a lower priority." -Josh Steimle, Entrepreneur and TEDx Speaker

4. **Exercise reduces stress.** Stress is a prevalent side-effect of running a business (unless your business is super-successful, but even that has its own stress that comes along with it). Regular exercise increases productions of endorphins that give you a natural high and bring about a calmer mindset to get you through the ups and downs of running a business.

5. **Exercise increases energy.** You don't need three cups of coffee each morning with an afternoon Red Bull chaser in order to keep energy high throughout the workday. A 2008 study published in the Journal Psychotherapy and Psychosomatics concluded that inactive individuals experienced increases in energy of up to 20 percent and decreased fatigue as much as 65 percent by participating in regular, low-intensity physical activity.

6. **Exercise boosts confidence to handle difficult tasks.** Confidence and fear avoidance are not constants in our lives. Sometimes we rise to the challenge with gusto while other times we lack the motivation to tackle life's hurdles. Why is there this discrepancy in our courage? Often times there is a chemical reason in our bodies that boosts or lowers our

confidence. Exercise tips that scale in your favor, bringing a capability to be more bold and achieve more.

"On my doctor's recommendation I started getting regular exercise. Not only did my health improve, but my business did as well. In fact, I'd say at this point that regular exercise is integral to my success as an entrepreneur." -Michael Hyatt, Entrepreneur & Author

7. **Exercise allows you to enjoy that life you are building for yourself.** Most entrepreneurs are working towards financial or lifestyle independence. However, while working hard for years while ignoring your physical health may lead you into these freedoms, your body will no longer be able to enjoy them to their fullest, or worse, your years will be numbered less because of your failing health. If you are going to build a cushy lifestyle for yourself, you might as well have a fit and capable body to enjoy it with.

How to Make the Exercise Habit Even Easier

So we've established why exercise is good for the business owner. Now let's focus on the "How":

1. **Make it the Highest Priority-** Treat exercise like your most important client. Schedule regular times and don't allow other interruptions to shift your commitment.

2. **Ignore How You Feel About It** - Once you have established

the habit of exercise, this gets easier. However, at the beginning, you aren't going to feel like doing it. That doesn't matter. Ignore your feelings and honor your commitment to yourself and your professional success.

3. **Find Something that You Enjoy** - Would you rather hike through the woods or take a bike ride? Would you rather play racquetball or wall climb? There are so many ways to get exercise that you might as well choose one that you enjoy the most.

4. **Make it Social** - We are way more likely to keep our commitments when there is a level of accountability. Find a parter that you can exercise with regularly or join a group class. You are more likely to stick with it when others are involved, and the workout is often more enjoyable.

Exercises You Can Do During the Workday

The Centers for Disease Control and Prevention recommends 30 minutes of moderate-intensity activity 5 times per week as part of a healthy lifestyle. In addition to this regular exercise time, entrepreneurs can benefit from mini-exercises sprinkled throughout their day.

If you use the Pomodoro Technique (working for 25 minute stretches with a 5 minute break), then throwing in one of these quick exercises is a great way to keep the oxygen flowing to your brain and preventing the fatigue caused by sitting for long periods, staring at a screen.

While pushups and sit-ups are great exercises you can do just about anywhere, you might find it awkward to get down on the ground during the middle of the workday. Alternatively, you can work out your legs and gluts, which are bigger muscles anyway, by doing lunges or standing squats. To most people, these just look like you are stretching which is much more socially acceptable in the workplace.

For the arms, you can also do wall-pushups. This involves standing a couple feet away from a wall and falling into it, then pushing yourself back out. This isn't going to build the biceps that other exercises will do, but it is a great way to get some blood flowing and engage muscles during a break in your afternoon.

One of best exercises to fit into your workday is to take a walk. It is so simple, yet often overlooked due to its simplicity. If you have one-on-one meetings, try to take them on a stroll instead of a meeting room. **Steve Jobs** was famous for his walking meetings, as is Facebook founder **Mark Zuckerberg**.

If you have to make a phone call that doesn't require sitting in front of your computer, do it with a headset while strolling.

Jack Dorsey, Cofounder of Square, takes all new hires at Square on a walk during their first Friday with the company. On this walk Dorsey takes the new hire through the streets of San Francisco, explaining the guiding principles behind Square.

Now, if you have your own office or don't have any qualms

about whipping out an exercise in the middle of your workday, then few things can get your heart-rate going faster than a minute of burpees, a total-body exercise.

Let's be honest, most readers knew that exercise was important before even reading this chapter. There's nothing ground-breaking here. However, even though we know this, we still aren't always motivated to action.

Perhaps a more effective mental picture is to imagine what your future looks like if you don't make time for exercise:

- Lower energy levels

- Less confidence

- Less creativity

- More stress

- Shorter lifespan

- More health problems as you age

Whenever we say "no" to something, we are saying "yes" to something else. The inverse is also true. Instead of looking at exercise as something you say "yes" to, think of it as saying "no" to the above items.

Making regular time for exercise seems like just one more thing to compete for your time during the day, but in the end, it could be the very thing that frees you up to achieve the success you are striving towards.

THE HABIT OF A MORNING ROUTINE

Have you ever found it easier to eat a healthy breakfast, while succumbing to temptation when it comes to evening snacks? Perhaps you find yourself more creative and productive in the morning hours, while the late afternoon is often punctuated by what many call a "slump". Whether your morning starts at 9:00am or 5:00am, the odds are that you find your best decision-making abilities and creativity strongest in the first part of your day.

Based off of anecdotal evidence, it would seem that we are primed to do our best work in the morning. Our sleep overnight rejuvenates us, our dreams help us process whatever is on our minds (consciously or unconsciously), so it makes a lot of sense that our best part of the day would be the morning. Because of this, it makes sense to have a deliberate plan to harness this magical part of the day, maximizing its potential, and setting the foundation for the rest of the day.

Remove the Decision Making Process

In the book *The Willpower Instinct*, the author explains how our ability to make good decisions slightly decreases with each decision we have to make. This may explain why at the end of the day we tend to cave into less desirable choices. If this is true, then it makes a lot of sense to remove certain decisions from our day that don't truly matter in the grand scheme of things:

- What am I going to wear today?

- What am I going to eat for breakfast?

- Should I check my email now or take a shower?

- Do I have time to work out?

All of these micro-decisions begin to eat away at our reserves for the day, and they are easily delegated to another time. For example, your outfit can be decided upon the night before, or better yet, you can adopt a personal uniform like Steve Jobs and wear the same thing every day. Facebook founder Mark Zuckerburg also wears the same shirt everyday in order to remove the process of deciding what to wear. Perhaps you can become a minimalist like Tim Ferriss, and reduce your wardrobe to just a few high-quality essentials.

For many of the other decisions, you can form a habit and

schedule, so the decision is not only made already, but you become used to the sequence so you can move effortlessly through the morning getting the most important items out of the way.

Give Yourself the Best of Yourself

Many financial planners tout the benefits of "Paying yourself first", or allocating a certain amount of funds to savings before you spend the rest on other expenses. The idea here is that you will be less tempted to splurge on that knick-knack instead of saving because the money has already left your bank account and is sitting in a savings vehicle. When it comes to managing our time, a similar principle applies:

Think of the most important activities you'd like to accomplish every day, and make those a priority above everything else that will interrupt your day.

Not only are you ensuring that these activities will be done each day, forming your desired habits, but they will also be done when you are at your peak.

Potential Activities to Avoid

Just like choosing the right activities for a morning routine, it is important to eliminate certain activities that can waste this important part of your day.

- **Morning News** - unless you have a good reason to pay attention to the morning news, your routine would do better to avoid hearing about all of the bad news that has happened overnight. Do you really need to start your day processing the domestic violence reported overnight, or the break-in across town? When you watch or read the news in the morning, you are giving someone else the opportunity to fill your mind with their agendas.

- **Your Phone** - Many of you are cringing at this one. I know, it's tempting to grab the phone off of my bedside stand and check email, tweets, messages, etc. before even leaving the bed. However, just like the morning news, by doing this I am giving someone else the opportunity to direct my attention and agenda for the morning. Try skipping the emails and notifications in the morning until after you've accomplished your routine.

- **Big Breakfast** - I know, I know, we're supposed to make breakfast the most important meal of the day. However, it is a fact that digestion takes energy, and eating a heavy meal has the effect of zapping our energy shortly afterwards. I definitely think that you should make a healthy breakfast a part of your morning routine, it just doesn't have to be a heavy platter of meats, eggs, potatoes, toast, butter, jam, etc. Try slimming that down to some fruit, or oatmeal, or egg whites with spinach. You'll still gain the nutritional benefit without the digestive overload.

- **Sleeping in on Weekends** - Weekends are for relaxing, right? Well our bodies have a circadian rhythm that is found throughout nature, that operates off of a 24-hour cycle. Basically, by waking up and going to bed at the same time, regardless of whether it is a weekday or weekend, our bodies become used to that pattern and will adjust accordingly. The more you keep consistency in your circadian rhythm, the easier it will be to awake and get started at the same time every morning. Even entrepreneur Richard Branson, when relaxing on his private island, still wakes up at 5:45 every morning.

Morning Ritual Activities:

- So, what exactly should our morning routine include? Well, that is going to depend a lot on the individual, and what they want to accomplish first during the day. The following are a suggested list to pick and choose from when building up your own morning routine.

- **Hydrate** - Our bodies lose over a pound of water every night as we sleep. This is primarily through the water vapor we exhale with every breath. To start the day off right, drink a full glass of water when you wake up to replenish.

- **Scrape Your Tongue** - I'm just going to assume that most people reading this are already brushing their teeth in the morning. However, I know that not many folks have taken up the habit of scraping their tongue, which disturbs and removes bacteria that builds up overnight. The result is fresher breath and healthier oral hygiene.

- **Stretch** - Even a few simple stretches can "wake up" the muscles in the body to start the day. Most of us stretch at least our arms into the sky when we yawn upon first waking up, why not follow through and give your midsection and legs a stretch as well?

- **Exercise** - For many people, if they don't exercise in the morning, it won't get done. Exercise also clears your mind for the day and gets the blood flowing, increasing your ability to make decisions and be creative. Even 10 minutes on a treadmill or a brisk walk around the block can make a huge difference in the start to your day.

- **Meditate** - You don't have to wear an eastern robe and learn how to chant in order to meditate. Meditation is simply the practice of clearing your mind, and learning how to focus. Founder of the Huffington Post, Arianna Huffington, starts every morning with 30 mins of meditation, she is so convinced of the benefits that she offers weekly classes to her employees.

- **Read Something Inspirational** - There are many "daily reader" type books that have a motivational thought for the day. Start your day off by taking a "emotional vitamin" to put things into perspective, and find some inspiration to stick with you throughout the day. You could also use this time to work through a business book, self-improvement book, or faith-based book.

- **Set/Review a Goal for the Day** - It is so easy to let the urgent, but unimportant activities invade our day. Take some time in the morning to review the day's goals, or perhaps a to-do list, and envision yourself completing that activity.

How to Get into the Habit

After you've decided what you are going to incorporate into a morning routine, the next step is to plan out your strategy for putting it into place. It's okay to start off with just one or two activities to commit to, and build from there. Some of the above activities might only take a couple of minutes. They don't have to be 30 minutes each to receive benefit from incorporating them into your morning.

- **Start by Getting Up 1 Hour Earlier** - If you normally get up at 8:00am, don't start by setting your alarm at 5:00am. Start with just an hour earlier, and if you find that you'd like to go earlier you can do it one hour at a time to ensure that you still feel rested (of course, your bedtime will likely adjust as well).

- **Write out a Plan the Night Before** - Don't go to bed without a plan. It is much harder to find motivation to start a morning routine when you are faced with the tiredness of waking up a little earlier. Make your plan the night before, write it down on a notecard, and focus on your *first step* on that card when you first wake up.

- **Prepare your Clothes, Journal, etc.** - I mentioned earlier that you might want to set out your clothes the night before. However, you can also set out your journal, your book, your tennis shoes, whatever you need to make the morning routine a success. You're much more likely to follow through when barriers are removed, however small.

- **Don't Be Discouraged by Slip-Ups** - My last piece of advice is to not get too hard on yourself. We all slip up sometimes, and the dangerous reaction is to just give up. Keep trying and you'll eventually find it hard *not* to do your morning routine.

THE HABIT OF MEETING WITH A MASTERMIND GROUP

About a year ago when I went into full-time entrepreneurship, I started hearing the word "mastermind" thrown around. At first it conjured up thoughts of an evil genius who is the mastermind behind some sort of catastrophe, but of course, the business world has another definition and use for the term.

Mastermind Group Definition

A mastermind group is simply a meeting of highly motivated folks who share a common goal and are looking to encourage and help each other improve.

That's basically the definition of what we talk about when we talk about business mastermind groups (shortened to "mastermind group" from here on out). These meetings can be in person, but they don't have to be. Mastermind meetings can also be online or over the phone.

Who Invented Mastermind Groups?

Mastermind groups have been around for a long time, but the phrase "mastermind group" was first coined by Napoleon Hill in his book *Think and Grow Rich*. According to Hill, a mastermind group is a "co-ordination of knowledge and effort, in a spirit of harmony, between two or more people, for the attainment of a definite purpose."

Some well-known examples of mastermind groups throughout history (even though they may not have been called that at the time) include:

- **The Junto** - Established in 1727 by Benjamin Franklin, The Junto initially consisted of 12 members who met together for mutual improvement by discussing moral, political, and scientific topics of the day.

- **The Inklings** - In the 1930's and 1940's, a group of English authors met together to read and discuss the author's unfinished works. Notable members include C.S. Lewis, J.R.R. Tolkien, and Owen Barfield.

- **Nine Old Men** - A group of Disney animators that were responsible for many of Disney's hits from 1930-1970. Classics such as *Peter Pan, Cinderella*, and *Alice in*

Wonderland were birthed in these meetings.

Whether the group is meeting for professional, political, or inspirational reasons, successful people have been meeting together in group collaboration for centuries.

Mastermind Group Agenda

There is no one way to run a mastermind group. However, it is important to have a structure, to ensure that everyone's time is respected and the group achieves its purpose of growth for its members.

The following is an example of the "Hot Seat Method" I learned from entrepreneur Pat Flynn:

- **Recap** - Each member updates the group on how they did accomplishing their goals from the previous meeting. The purpose here is not to go into too much detail or probe, but simply have that accountability of vocalizing out loud how you did.

- **Hot Seat** - A chosen member will share details about their situation, and any problems or questions that they have can arise during this time. The other members of the group then have the opportunity to provide specific help and advice to this individual.

- **Goal Setting** - Similar to the "recap", each member will go around and briefly state their goals for the next meeting.

- **Hot Seat Selection** - The next person to become the "hot seat" is selected, so they can come prepared with questions or concerns to bring before the group.

This method ensures that each person has the chance to participate, and only one person gets to dominate the conversation for a time in order to deep-dive into their current concerns. By rotating through the members, each one will get a chance to hear advice from the other members on their specific situation.

An alternative method that has been laid out by Chris Ducker is to distribute the focus during the meeting to each member as opposed to a hot seat. In order to achieve this, each member has to share the following:

- Something that is working well for them.

- Something that they would like help with.

- A resource (website, app, service, blog post) to share with the group.

Ducker shares another tip of utilizing a Google Doc that everyone in the group has read/write access to during the meeting to collaborate on notes. Another interesting fact about Ducker's mastermind is that it lasted several hours, so it was not a weekly event.

I think this sort of extended mastermind meeting is great for making a huge impact, and gaining some momentum that can last several months. Recently Barrett Brooks wrote about a "mastermind retreat" that he took with the members of his group. He explains how they normally meet weekly for a short time, but were looking for something more:

"Meeting for an hour a week or 90 minutes every two weeks allows us to stay up to date and hold each other accountable, but it doesn't allow for deep understanding of each other's businesses or comprehensive business planning." -Barrett Brooks

Brooks also comments on how virtual meetings can grow dull over time, and the energy level of the group can take a hit without the occasional physical meeting.

However the agenda of the group plays out, again it is important that the time is spent intentionally, and that everyone gets an equal opportunity to seek help from the rest of the group.

The Benefits of a Mastermind Group

It is the temptation of many entrepreneurs and consultants to try to go it all alone. However, as poet John Donne wrote in the 17th century: "No man is an island". By tapping into the minds of several like-minded individuals, a group member experiences the following benefits:

- Accountability to think ahead and make a plan until the next meeting

- Accountability to act upon that plan

- Feedback and constructive criticism from others who want to see you succeed

- Insight you might not have otherwise gained

- Access to new resources

- Motivation to grow and avoid stagnation

It's true, participating in a mastermind group takes time and energy, but the clarity and insight it provides is time well spent.

Why Mastermind Groups Work

When you plug into a network of people with similar goals and the desire to help each other, you plug into something that you aren't likely to get any other way. When you expose yourself to a mastermind group, you benefit from the differing perspectives of the other group members, which bring about insight that you otherwise wouldn't have been privy to.

Entrepreneur and author Timothy Ferriss states: "I don't think people need more motivation. I think they need more feedback and accountability, that's it." I would venture to say that feedback and accountability, such as what is found in a mastermind group, tend to provide the type of motivation that makes a difference.

Where to find a Mastermind Group

Mastermind groups are everywhere, and certainly many are occurring online and are open to new members. The quickest way to find a mastermind group is to visit the MasterMinds Meetups (http://masterminds.meetup.com/) page on meetup.com. Here you will find a map and listing of mastermind groups around the world.

However, as I've stated earlier, the best masterminds consist of folks with similar goals. If one person is an aspiring author while another is looking to reduce churn on his SaaS application, the two might not have as much in common as would be ideal for a mastermind setting.

In order to find like-minded individuals who are open to forming a mastermind group (or know of one you might be able to join), you can check the following sources:

- **Twitter** - Engage with people around a certain hashtag or interest topic. Tweet out that you are interested in joining a mastermind group for your particular niche.

- **Forums** - Find a forum where people in your situation are hanging out, and look for mastermind opportunities there.

- **Blog Comments** - I've read more than one interaction where someone comments on a post and asks for advice on joining a mastermind on that topic, and others follow up with similar interests as comment replies.

- **Facebook/LinkedIn Groups** - Groups on these social networks are often a great way to meet like-minded people and look around for mastermind opportunities.

- **Conferences** - By networking at conferences you can make connections with others interested in your particular niche, and looking to meet as a mastermind group.

Of course, if you poke around and can't find a mastermind group with your particular niche or in your area, then it's time to start one!

Starting a Mastermind Group

Every mastermind group is started by someone. Why not you? All it takes is one other person to get a mastermind group started. Of course, in order to have a successful group meeting, a few key items must be discussed amongst the founding members:

- **Pick a Topic** - State specifically what this mastermind group is going to be about. Be as specific or general as you'd like, knowing that the more specific the focus the stronger the growth in that area will be.

- **Pick the Ground Rules** - Will there be consequences for so many missed meetings? Will there be a time limit? Come up with a few of these foundational rules to ensure that everyone is on the same page, and they all know what they are signing up for.

- **Chose the Agenda** - Again, having an agenda will keep the meeting moving and show respect for everyone's time. This doesn't have to be set in stone, perhaps it will evolve over time, but never start a meeting without an agenda.

- **Keep an Eye out for New Members** - Many masterminds are invite-only, and for good reason. You want your mastermind group to maintain a high level of focus and to be filled with other motivated individuals. Some masterminds even have an application and interview process to join, while others grow only with recommendations from existing members.

Once the topic, ground rules, and agenda are discussed, then it's time to meet! During the meetings, it is important not to interrupt (which can happen more often than we realize), and give each person an equal chance to share and give feedback. Another topic to discuss is whether or not the meeting will be captured, either by written notes or a recording.

Like many other successful entrepreneurs, you can elevate your success by starting or joining a mastermind group. Entrepreneur Pat Flynn writes:

"I would not be where I'm at today if it weren't for the mastermind groups that I've been a part of since I began doing business online." -Pat Flynn

Whether you are stuck in a rut, on a plateau, or experiencing slow growth, a mastermind group can provide the boost in energy, new perspectives, accountability, and resources necessary to take your game to the next level.

CONCLUSION

Thanks for reading *The 9 Habits of Successful Entrepreneurs*. If you haven't had the chance, head over to https://ryanbattles.com/5-habits to download the bonus content: *The 5 Habits that Derail You as an Entrepreneur*.

Also, I'd love to hear your thoughts on the book! Please consider leaving a review on Amazon so I can hear what people find useful.

As I mentioned in the introduction, these habits are not going to be easy to implement, but are well worth the time and effort in putting them into practice. If these were simple to implement, then millionaire entrepreneurs would be the norm instead of the outliers.

Where do you see yourself 2 years from now? The place you

will be in the near future is greatly influenced by the small decisions you make today, tomorrow, the day after, etc. Let this be the year that you see hockey stick growth in your success, put the right habits into place that empower you to go beyond your goals and achieve breakout success.